Words

That

Kill

Words

That

Kill

Vivid Vega

Creating a new style of
poetry, Vivid Vega includes
a hidden poem within
poems, calling it Vivid.

Poetry includes drawings
from the author.

Follow Vivid Vega on Instagram:

@VividVega

25% of every purchase goes to anti- cruelty organizations.

For more information visit @ProtectPups on Instagram

For the one who

brings me light

in the darkness

Table of Contents

Sticks and Stones

Sticks and Stones may break

bones, but words will forever kill

me

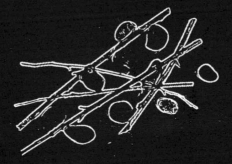

I am forever killed by words
in my mind
I am forever killed by the
words people speak that
aren't kind
I have kept the pain inside
But they break free and can no
longer hide

The *pain* is like sticks
rooting to my skin

It hurts as hard as
stones *within*

You are the
heavy pain
in my
throat
clotting my
words only
able to
express
itself into
tears
-the
breaking
point

The repeating

thought of what

could've been

haunts my mind

-the what ifs

I am lonely and I wish to be
revived

But I *am* the darkness because my
light has died

I am *not* what people want to see

I am not good *enough* so people
try and change me

I dream of *nothing* coming out
from my voice when I try and
shout. I never *remember* what my
dreams are about. So I stay *awake*
at night with my mind clouded
with doubts.

People try and create this distorted image of me. Coldness in my eyes is all they see. They *don't* understand that my coldness is actually me being shy. People don't *understand* me so instead they say goodbye. People I have used. My heart is now bruised. All I ever wanted was to be good enough, but I cannot be. People think of *me* as less so I try and be tough, but that is not me.

The world demises with my pen
at hand

The *world* dissolves when my
mind they try and understand

The world
disintegrates
to my voice
like the
grains of
sand

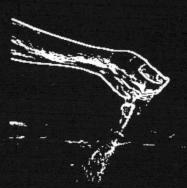

People try and *tear* me apart

They don't know the pain masked
in *my* heart

I wish my *name* they did not
mention

But I'm brought *up* like a
connection

I *never* ask
people how
they are in

fear of getting asked in return

They cause my heart to burn

So I mask my name

So they don't have *anyone* to
blame

No matter the hits he gives you
from his lips, I will always be
here for you.

-Unrequitted Love

The monsters are *taking* over my mind

Sanity I try and find

But they come through the shadows of *my* mind and take over my being

Until the light of *clarity* in my eyes is no longer what I'm seeing

They drown me *with* voices

They are the reason for all of my *choices*

I am not bulletproof and your
words shot me to the deepest
depths of my core

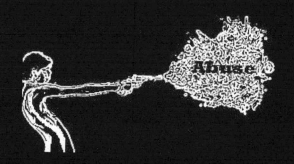

"Why are you so ugly?" He
asked as I squeezed my juicebox
while it splattered in my hands
from the *painful* beginning of
the *thought* that'll forever haunt
me *of* thinking I will *never* be
good *enough*.

-How it started

The darkness creeps into *my* skin

It seeps deep in my *mind* within

It *is* waiting to write itself into a poem

My *darkness* has found the light of its new home

I will always remember what *you*
did and said
It's stuck inside my head
They *are* the reason I wish I was
dead
But I am *suffering* in my mind
instead
All I feel is dread
This misery won't end
Since the day you forced *me* onto
your bed

You are the waves of heat

While *I* am
the snow

You melt me
like *defeat*

Until there's
nothing left to
show

I so badly have wanted to hear you say you *love* me, but you never did which destroyed me. Like how the boundless whispers in *the* wind destroys the silence of a broken heart within. Now all you hear in my heart are echoes of *silence*, and it breaks from your heartless violence.

To have the world on the tip of
your fingers but death engraved
on your skin is such a blessed
cursed but I don't know which is
worse

Not even *the* river can wash away
my *past*

It *makes* me
shiver thinking it
would never last

Now *my* mind
keeps on
haunting me

With *memories*
that keep
taunting to be *free*

I cannot *forgive* my wrongs or
rights
The decisions are blurring *my*
sight
For my *sanity* I
hold on tight
I am not ready
to let go *tonight*

I look at the window of the train to see
my reflection
I see strangers sitting in silence like
we're all in connection
We don't say a word to one another for
the sake of our "protection"
But when a word slips out we pretend
to not pay attention
We all crave affection
But we all look another direction

The world is filled with silent cries
I look out as the train passes by
I see your reflection staring into my
eyes
Our words are hidden like the sun
covered by the clouds in the sky
The world is filled with hidden lies
So we sit in silence without a hello
or a goodbye

I am falling into despair

I wish I could be invisible like
the air

But I am like a firework ready to
ignite

How I wish I too could
disappear into the darkness of
the night

There are so many colors around

But black and white *is* all she sees

The skyline reflects *no* light in her eyes

The world is infinite with no size

Radiance is what you see shining

She sees no *light* in the stars aligning

She shines beautifully but feels so blue

Because for her there's no hue

A pen and a paper is all I need

My pen goes through the paper

the way my wrists bleed

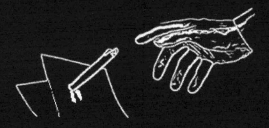

You say you want to get to know
who I am

But when I *reach* out you never
grab my hand

It's like climbing *up* a ladder while
you're holding it below

Than looking down and *you're*
face is *nowhere* to show

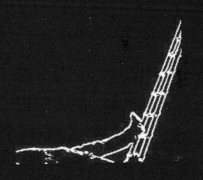

How do you expect one to move
on when our whole lives we've
been told that love lasts forever?

You're the leaves in autumn

Always changing until you
break

Always *grabbing* until you get
to the bottom

Until there's *nothing* left to take

I am *masked* with
pain
I am no longer who
I used to be
How can I *keep* sane
When you took my
identity *away* from
me

They say *I* am thin

But the my eyes will *never* win

I wish I could *see* clearer

But I see more pounds on *me*
when I look in the mirror

He scarred my lips
I can no longer
speak
The venom drips
I've become weak

It's too late to be saved because I
am weak
I'm ashamed of who I am and can
no longer speak
I wish to be a shadow but I am not
invisible
Because I can be seen, I wish I was
divisible
So I can split in different pieces
and hide away
I wish I had the
strength to have
something to say
But I live inside of my
brain
And now my thoughts
are slowly going insane

Last breath

To the words that bring one to their
last breath

These are words that bring one to
the edge of death

To the words that bring blood on
one's hands

To the ones who have no one that
understands

One last breath
that I show
The words are
haunting me
everywhere I go
I can no longer
speak
My tongue has
become weak

The venom goes to my
blood

Towards my *heart* it does
flood

It *drowns* me with pain

Poetry is the only way the
venom can drain

I have blood on my lips *tonight*
Because *I* have been bitten by
my shame
My demons *have* come into
sight
And they're ready *to* take over
my good name
No matter how much I try and
fight
They cause me to go insane
So I hopelessly try and find *the*
light
But these *demons* can't be
tamed

He strikes me like a bat with his
fists
And tells me sorry with a
bouquet of gifts

-Stand up to abuse

You have the
ability to
engrave my
name on a
tombstone

You drain my
blood and
disintegrate my every bone

You take away my independence
so I feel alone

You ripped me up to pieces so I
have never grown

I was atoms and cells turned to
stone

You put me in your dungeon
when you declared the throne

I feel like *I* jumped off the bridge and *changed* my mind too late to save *myself*... What have I become?

All I have to remember you by is
memories but they begin to fade
away

Just like the last words *I* ever
heard you say

I *feel* so alone

With you I wish I could have
grown

I hope
heaven *is*
treating
you well

But your coffin was the last *time*
I'd see you since I'm going to hell

I will never be good

enough for anyone

No matter how

hard I try

I've never had the chance to have a childhood. Why I didn't have friends no one understood. I was sheltered from the danger outside. But my parents never knew the demon was inside.

I was forced to work while I was young. To not have a single friend is why my heart stung. Why are you so ugly? Is what kids would ask. So I grew up without a voice and my pain I'd mask.

My pain grew stronger. I didn't know how much I could take much longer. I was reborn through poetry. Until one day someone decided to force me. I tried jumping off the bridge of my school. But to traumatize people with my dead body would make me a fool.

And again I am alone.
I will never escape this dark zone.
I wish differently I couldve grown.
But soon my name will be on a tombstone.

There are no happy endings while
I lay in the coffin of *my* mind
There is no sanity or *light* for me to
find
I am forever stuck inside
This will be the place they find my
poetry
has
died

I tried to drain you from the
wavering blood in my skin

I *tried* to wash it away by the
blade but it would never win

I tried *to* get you out of my mind
because you make me *feel* ill

But my eyes always open from the
blackouts caused by each pill

Like a flower

I will bloom again

-Depression

A root growing from the ground is now I feel
When I grow up, will I be ideal?
I've fallen so deep into the rabbit hole
The thoughts are rooted into my soul
And I dig deeper to make me feel whole
But digging only makes it emptier until there's nothing left to show
Is it possible to become complete?
I don't want to experience defeat
Like the stones in the ground once you step that'll hurt
I don't want to be the ground they step on like dirt

I dare not to speak on what has *caused* my heart to become so weak and why I can never fall asleep. So instead I stay awake as I rest my head and lay on my bed wishing the *pain* of wanting to be dead would end.

Inside I am breaking, how can I
repair? My mind is shaking, I
think it's the despair. I am not
treated fair. I wish to become
invisible like the air. But even the
air could be felt. I wish my
demons could be dealt. I am not a
pretty face because I am a
nightmare. People say I put them
in a trance from the way I stare. I
am not a pretty sight. I am the
demons
crawling
around in the
darkness of
the night.

He locks his car door and won't let me out until he gives me a "ride"

Our visions
of eternity
are in *exile* of
our minds

What one
sees isn't always what one finds

We destroy one another in fire

We are brainwashed by the demon
of desire

Our demise has no escape

We've *created* a world with a hero
without a cape

We will continue *to* dance around
infernal concerts

Because we are too blind to see they
are the inventions of the *monsters*

They say communication is key

So why is it that you hear Yes
when I
say,
don't
touch
me?

I can never be what people say. I stay up late at night afraid to start a new day. I *have* never been happier when I *ignored* everyone and became what I wanted. But everyone's criticism has *my* mind haunted. I no longer speak. They have driven me to the point that I am weak. I can no longer sleep. In my *mind* now they are too deep.

Your *eyes* demise lies from the
blue skies and ties its *wavering*
blue color like a dance *to* my heart
and the only way I'll look away is
if you tear *me* apart

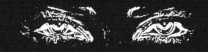

I cannot speak
I *am* too weak

My blood
starts to leak
so the light I
seek

Where is my head? I think I'm
dead

I wish you were *here* instead

I wish I didn't leave things
unsaid

All *I* did with their hearts is break
them so mercilessly. I didn't mean
to do this purposely. I wanted
someone to worship me, but I
destroyed
them in the
process so
perfectly.

Karma has stricken me with a
vengeance like a
riptide

All I wanted was
happiness by my
side

But karma has risen
into a hurricane

And now my mistakes *can't* be
washed away by the rain

They won't go away

I cannot *change* what I say

So I die inside

And now there is nowhere to *hide*

Do not teach boys and girls that causing *pain* means to love or be loved.
Teach them that love is not pain, because yes love *is* powerful, but no it is not *abuse*.

-He pushes you because he likes you

She was merely a shadow on the ground I so desperately tried to grasp onto unreachable ends. She *was* always in sight so I dug towards the core of the earth but she was *intangible*. While I was the wind, invisible, *but* able to be felt in such a bitter transition from a sweet summer breeze to a vengeful uprising gust of a hurricane. *I* desired to be seen by the unreachable and in the end the darkness of her shadow *was* more powerful than the whirling winds *drifting* me more *away* from her.

You burn me with your desire

And I am not fireproof

Burn me with your attire

Let *me*
melt for
you

Women
carry the
strength on
their backs
to lift each
other up, so
why do we
tear one
another
down like
bulldozers?

I favor vision over how I *feel*. That's
why everything is dark and *nothing* is
real, and why I
couldn't see the fire
in my heart so other
hearts I'd steal.

I lick your venom off *my* lips

I used to *love* the way it drips

But now I am immune

You *vanished* from my
bloodstream so soon

Now you leave my lips *with*
nothing to say

So evaporate and find yourself
another prey

My lips tremble yes

But my heart *screams* no

I let *you* touch me as I undress

But my heart feels *empty* and cold

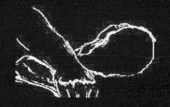

To see the buildings of the city,
every morning *I* look out the
windows of the train

But the city has *lost* its color, or
perhaps it's all in *my* brain

Maybe I've been driven to
madness through sorrow, but I
don't want to be insane

To jump out the doors *into*
oblivion, my *thoughts* can't refrain

I am trying hard to repair
But *everything*
rips like a tear
I wish together I
could be joint
But it is
impossible, since
this *is* my
breaking point

At dusk I stare at the city *lights* on

the bridge that

gleam

My *eyes* know

everything isn't

what it seems

We all *look* different on the

outside *but* we are rooted for the

same *destiny*

Because one day the bridges *will*

fall and the lights will *burn* out

until there's nothing left of *you* or

me

The *pain* is coming in stronger

To the point I *can't* feel any longer

This sensation is
forever here to *stay*

It's been in my
limbs since you've
been *away*

I stay up at night now that I
can't *sleep*

Because I've done
things my lips
cannot bare to
speak

I try and find a
shadow of *light*

But my past keeps haunting *me*
to stay *up* at night

I look so vibrant, but inside I am
empty
I question everyday why my
colors have *left* me
I am a *dying* rose whose bright red
color faded *into* a blackish brown
I am the *darkness* of the ocean
ready to drown

To drive *into* oblivion my
thoughts can't refrain

But I am only driven into *madness*
and I am going insane

To *crash* into your heart would be
my greatest pleasure

I'd steer into the abyss for you at
any measure

I See the Light

No matter the shadows of the night

In the darkness you can find a light

For the ones who only see the

darkness of the abyss

My words are your light when you

experience this

The lights that shine in my dark
mind
There is always a light that one
can find
When you think the light has died
You can find the light inside

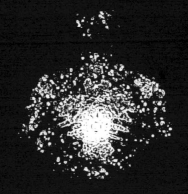

For you, I'd give up my
ability to rhyme

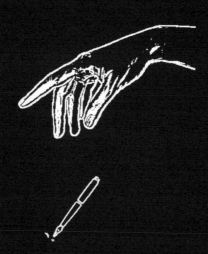

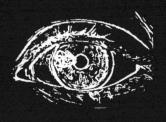

The light is a
disguise

We are blinded
from our eyes
of the *world's* lies

We don't see there is *only*
darkness in the light

We are *blinded* by the vision the
world provided for our sight

We walked right past one another

Not knowing we were meant for eachother

-Missed Connections

I am a million shades of darkness

I am only afraid of losing the sun inside

of me

Because I don't want to be invisible like

the wind

Or as dark as a shadow

But I am no more than a paradox

Because I too am intangible

When someone reaches out for me, I

push them away as heavy as the winds

of a hurricane

I don't want the lights of others inside

of me, which is what

I was blinded by

Because all I needed

was to create a fire

inside of myself

I loved you when you first I saw
I would protect
you and hold
your paw
You are my best
friend
I will be by your
side until the end

Without your breed, life would
halt its speed, there would be no
point to proceed, because without
you I'd rather bleed, since you're
the only best friend I need.

-Man's bestfriend

My dearest Rose

My heart you stole

You're like a book of prose

Writing yourself into my soul

The *words* I speak

The ocean turning

You *make* me weak

Yet you're the one I'm yearning

Your tides crash into my skin

Your *eyes* the ocean blue

Your waves are crashing me
within

But I would *drown* without you

Your bones and *blood* will one
day fade away
Just like the diamonds and stars
you see today
Because everything *fades* into the
abyss
So make life last as you read this

The lights are *inside* of me
They *are* trying to break free
My heart grows colder by the day
I imprison *my* thoughts by things I
don't say
My *demons* are breaking out of
their cage
I don't know how much my mind
can wage
And now I *will*
expel so bright
But all they
wanted was for
me to *be* as *silent*
and mysterious as
the night

The quest is best when
you don't let me rest and
treat me as your guest
when you serve *me* with
your body *undressed*

You have the ability to *make* me

feel expressive and romantic,

you leave *me* feeling frantic and

I'm feeling like *your addict*

because you're electricity *while*

I'm your static and you got me

feeling ecstatic

so *my heart*

you can have

it.

Dance with the
darkness of my
shadows *in* the
night
Let it bring you a
midst of light
Or wait for *the* rays
of the *moonlight* so
I'm what you're
seeing
Grab me by the hips
and dance with my
being

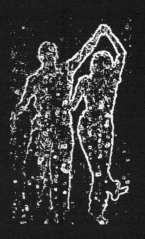

I've been caught by a string of motion

Ready to *cut* loose and dissolve into devotion

My blood wavers like a melody

And my *words* are captivated breathlessly

I've been ice but my cold heart turned *into* fire

And I crave *her* being with a burning sense of desire

Not even the

world could flood

the earth the way

your tongue
wavers

between my legs

The darkness *inside* covers my
spirit

The *light* that shines inside of me,
I *will* not fear it

It yearns to *be* free

But it is the *darkness* I don't want
you to see

It seems like it's *filling* inside of
me

But it's not what it looks to be

It'll explode deep
in *my* zone

It's so dark in my
mind, I don't want
to be alone

I grab her hips
and kiss her lips
and hold her
hand as she says
she's never had a
love like this with
any other man

I want to be a part of your towers

And I *want* to be wrapped in the
city when it starts *to* shower

I want to *be* a part of the reflection
of the famous bean

And be on the peak of the sky
deck allowing *everything* to be
seen

I want *to* have your city lights on
me shine

I don't want the lights to burn out
because I want *you* to be mine

103

Not even the rain
can touch your
skin when I'm
with you
You keep me
sane when you
are in the
umbrella with
just us two

I feel the
rush of
liquids
pour out
of me

Suddenly it gets more blurry and
hard for me to see

I *feel* my cells scatter and my mind
feels blank

I think that even my heart sank

The room gets dark and I am *free*

Now I see and I'm not who I used
to be

You are a portal
of life

-Women

The fibers that make up *my* being

Are *fading* into the abyss without seeing

Because we don't realize we are all rooted for the same *destiny*

In the end we fade away into a memory

My cells are scattered my head *is* gray

I liberate the *eternity* of who I am today

There is only *darkness* inside of my mind. A tint of color is what *I* try and *find*. I looked for light *in* others who were kind. There was a fire in *my heart* I could not see from being too blind.

We are *masked* by the identities
we try and portray

We mask the things that we truly
want to say

Our light breaks through when we
are true

For you *to* judge me I ask, who are
you?

We are all under *control* but are
too blind to see

We are surrounded by *the*
darkness of *society*

There is no
need to hide in
the shade

The light will
come and your
pain will fade

Despite the hits and the many
times *you* have been forced to
please while on your knees just
know you *are* not a tease when
you could not say no since the
pain made you freeze

No matter the times you tried to
take your life away

Remember that you are strong and
that is why you are standing here
today

There is always light somewhere
even if you're in too much *pain* to
see

Just know that sooner or later the
pain *will* fade and set you free

Even if you can't see it and it tries
to *tear* you apart

There will always
be a light for *you*
to feel inside of
your heart

Follow Vivid Vega on
Instagram:

@VividVega

25% of every purchase goes
to anti- cruelty organizations.

Fore more information visit
@ProtectPups on Instagram

52416942R00068

Made in the USA
San Bernardino, CA
19 August 2017